# Love After Love
## Has Failed

Poems by John P. Asling

THE CHOIR PRESS

Editing: Vicky Morris
Design: growords@gmail.com

First published in the United Kingdom in 2024 by
The Choir Press.

CP
THE CHOIR PRESS

ISBN: 978-1-78963-443-3

*To all those who dare to love –*
*even after love has failed*

'Take down the love letters from the bookshelf,
the photographs, the desperate notes, peel
your own image from the mirror. Sit.
Feast on your life.'

From *Love After Love* by Derek Walcott

# Contents

# Body and Soul

I am body,
searching for soul.
All this living
is taking its toll.

My broken limbs,
these hidden bruises.
All this dying
one never chooses.

Perfect moments
of passion, bliss.
All this loving
my skin will miss.

Now here are signs
of rapid decay.
All this searching,
I must not delay.

# Waves

You send me that shock postcard from Paris,
the Arc de Triomphe etched against a blue sky,
the Champs Elysee somehow free of traffic,
your scribble responding to my dare,
to traverse the deep Atlantic Ocean.

I phone from the noisy newsroom – the editor yelling,
Rewrite it or we spike it! I can't hear you at all. Did you
say yes? I'm still not sure. Yet, we go out, to Toronto's
Poor Alex – Urbania, a futuristic drama – wondering
what lies ahead. You ignore the drink I buy you.

There's no kiss at your door, a gentleman, you think,
or, do you? I'm not sure. I don't want to ruin things,
ruin us. More chaste dates follow, then I take off,
hitchhike West, tempted by the sultry Vancouver poet,
return weeks later, drift towards marriage, praying

love follows. You wear the pink floral dress, sewn
by your sister, finished moments before you walk
down the aisle of ageing Saint Dunstan's, clutching
a June bouquet, while Frank and Charlie sing Love,
look at the two of us, strangers in many ways.

The letter you write me after I leave twenty years later
admits you didn't yet love me on our wedding day –
the vows we wrote, the priest's perfect preaching, plans
we'd made notwithstanding – but you insist love did
grow over time, and I squandered it. I tear the letter

to shreds – but can't argue it. And today I weep,

hearing that song exactly fifty years later,
scribble you a post-love letter, a lament, a poem,
from England's side of the fathomless ocean.
But I don't send it. It's too late sadly, still strangers –

the waves of life only carry us further apart.

# Missing the Great White North

The books you sent arrived today,
fresh accounts of the Canadian fray.

I'll put them aside until I finish my Joyce,
but swear I can hear my country's sweet voice.

Not just the words of Francis or Toews,
nor our sad sagas of descendant slaves,

but the prairies and mountains of a former life,
fragmented memories of kin, and a now ex-wife.

They've followed me here to this England home,
where I'm gently settled, no longer to roam.

The fresh ink of these pages helps me embrace
the scent of nostalgia for friendship and place.

The dead and the dying, the living far away,
are here in this garden of sunshine and clay.

# Strong Winds

*for Ian & Sylvia*

Can't sing that song,
today or tomorrow,
it's all gone wrong.

Can't listen in,
from here or there,
just can't win.

Winds won't
blow strong, seas
don't run high,

weather's not good,
night's too long.
Won't fly

in snow, or wait
for change, so lonely now,
staying straight.

Sung far away,
I hear that tune,
pray you'll say –

Please come soon.

# Bring Your Love

Cross the ocean,
bring your love.

Waves in motion,
God's above.

Float like clouds,
gently touch.

Sing it aloud,
joy and such.

Sisters splitting
at the seam.

Mother's quitting
widow's dream

Prayers from heaven,
drunk as hell.

Family's leaven,
lost its spell.

Cross the ocean,
bring your grief.

Silent notion,
rests beneath.

Taste the water,
salt and deep.

End the slaughter,
rest in sleep.

# Learning How to Tell the Time

Cradle time –
   split lip,
      mouth of muck.

Toddler time –
   crushed fine
by market truck.

Youth time –
   harsh pucks
      and sharp sticks.

Wound time –
   no stitches
      could ever fix.

# Toronto Childhood

Still, his angry belt makes
a quaking fool of me.

Seeking pleasure
from infirmity.

His pain, my daily
bread or scarcity.

I turn his lashes
into stinging poetry,

until words run
out of symmetry.

Still, what of those
midnight ministries,

my cough so loud
it could wake the devil.

His spoonful
of healing honey,

a rare sweet
on a bitter night.

# The Love We Cherish –

Soiled mornings.
The daily walk of dread.
His leather strap across my backside.
Stupid.
Clumsy.

Her broken ribs.
Muffled cries.

His crash-car ladies.
Smashed.

Brothers wrapped in napkins, bows.
Sisters warped in fear.

The love we cherish –
is not here.

# Mantras

Brothers in brown,
white cords around.

Latin bellows
from holy fellows.

Paul sings aloud
John floats on a cloud.

Sole in our ears.
Bells calm all fears.

Away at school,
praying by rule.

Visiting Days,
family frays.

Cakes and treats,
boasting of feats.

Tears at front door,
Mom off to war.

Back to textbooks,
treats from the cooks.

Nights without dreams,
not yet fourteen.

# Summer of '69

Love rocked the hood,
the moon dusted our feet,
your lips said I should,
we collapsed in the heat.

We drank up our youth,
grazed in sweet gardens green,
tasted flavours uncouth –
God, we were keen.

It was I'm Ok, You're Ok,
our clothes we forgot,
and Lay Lady Lay –
Aquarius besot.

That sweet living for loving,
dying didn't exist,
the poetry was nothing –
we couldn't resist.

# State of Mind

Trains of yellow spray in February's
slush on sensible tourist shoes.

They hurry past a cardboard plea:
penned in black: Help, I'm HIV.

Stoned teens cart babies down
slippery subway steps towards

the beating of Mother Earth's heart,
ground zero to ancient ones,

whose cry for justice
is lost, amid rising monuments

to naked bigotry, returned in kind
a hundred times, while

the Statuesque One watches over
her city of glass and glare,

where sleep is not welcome,
but every street's named Liberty.

# Venice

I am searching
your misty waterways,
ancient alleyways,
holy squares.

Still,
the future
is nowhere
to be seen.

I am lost –
in the depths
of your canals,
your unending streets,
wide open piazzas.

Map-less,
in the moment
of our present
love.

# Best of Times

It's that most perfect time of day,
when the sun steps out to wash
the rain away. You're home,
so I'm inclined to stray
from wired space to garden
green with clay. Sipping tea
with stories milked from the fray.

It's that most perfect time of night,
when the moon is in its bedclothes,
tucked in tight, and you're here
lying warm beside me, before our souls
take flight, from whispers to yawping
godly delight, we taste the sweet fruit
of our bodies' summiting heights.

It's that most perfect time of year,
the clouds conspire to hide my raging fear.
Your hand's inclined to hold me
close and dear, from morning to night,
the truth sings clear: loving remains
within the holy sphere.

# Walking With You at 7am

Early next day we walk
together, for the first time,
around the lake locals called Leman,
though ex-pats know it as Geneva.

It's a cold January morning, the wind
off the lake stinging our pale skin.
Are you a hand holder? I ask.
I don't know. Let's see. She says.

I reach out in time with our strides
and take her nurse's hand in mine:
Thinking of all the limbs it's gently held,
the people it's helped to heal.

There'll be months of red wine
in her old Paquis flat, bacon, scrambled eggs,
Kristofferson crooning melancholy
on her tiny CD player.

Never a kiss, or a night stayed over.
Too soon or too late, we wonder, while happy
to wander the old town, and ponder both
Leonard and Lucinda, music that feeds us,

the slap of politics, country and family,
retreating to the smoky jazz club
where we first met, to hear the hypnotic
hymns of the Cote D'Ivoire.

It will all be wildly insane.

And friends will say, Not again!
But our walking will be like praying –
for new chapters, love,

after love has failed. Two decades on,
we walk by the sea, sometimes it rains,
but no matter - the time of day or the weather -
her damp hand holds me still closer.

# Waiting For My UK Visa

Daydreaming a country
in a nightmarish state,
wasting my days
at an unholy rate,
wandering the streets
wondering my fate.

The paperwork's perfect,
but the shuffling's late,
it gathers in boxes,
soon filling a crate –
the government's busy,
it won't set a date.

Then a knock at the door,
a man at the gate,
he wants to sell pizza,
and add to my weight.
Another brings the post,
with bills to be paid.

It's not for me to love them,
and I'm not tempted by hate,
so I sit in the garden,
close my eyes and I wait.
The days go slowly,
the nights can't equate.

Been playing the game
since 2008,
first it was springtime,

it's now April 8th.
I'm daydreaming a country
in a nightmarish state.

# Once Upon a Star

Love in Goa.
It's a girl.
Amazing Girl.

Once upon eternity
in a universe at night,
your star shines through the darkness,
and sets the world alight.

Mummy's Girl. Daddy's Girl.
Everyone's favourite Girl.
Sparkling Girl.

Dancing Girl. Shopping Girl. Driving Girl.
World-travelling Girl. London Girl. New York Girl.
Where next Girl?

Working Girl. Studying Girl. Baby-sitting Girl.
Smart Girl. Beautiful Girl.
Girls just want to have fun Girl.

Dancing high on heaven's stage,
unleashing a world of delight,
the sparkle through your firmament,
blesses those with sight.

Mind of her own Girl.
Carefree Girl. Caring Girl.
Good in a crisis Girl. Brave Girl.

Grown up Girl.

Not just Girl.
No longer Girl.

Now Woman.
Wonder Woman.
The World's Waiting for this Woman.

You reveal just what joy is,
how it banishes the fright.
Dance on, dear star, dance on,
Jo-Eva – what a sight!

# On Moving Near the Sea

Turner skies are at our gate.
Boats steer home, drunk with freight.

Clouds of wrath will not wait.
Ships at sea tempting fate.

Winds so wild, shore's a state.
Safe home all, don't be late.

Storm is imminent at this rate.
Turner skies drown our gate.

# Andrew on the Balcony

His gaze is lost
at sea, dragging on
roll-your-own morbidity.

Inhaling his preferred
reality, oblivious
to land's frothing waters,

the lifeboats' bleak beckoning
beneath the balcony.
Disconnected

from waves of rich memories –
that have scrambled
his body's very symmetry.

His gaze is lost
at sea, but dry land,
is a shrinking island.

# Ocean

Mother waves,
crashes,
carries,
bitter-cold brine
to me.

Mother washes,
flashes,
ferries,
wild foaming sea
from me.

Mother waits,
watches,
wonders,
what's to become -
of me.

# Zimbabwe Memories

She sits before me,
black, smooth, immovable,
a rock.

Perhaps a majesty,
mysterious, magnetic,
to be feared.

She reaches back,
her neck straining,
toward the past.

Remembering what?
Ghosts of oppression?
Wisps of revolutionary joy?

Her dark eyes stare,
dead ahead, capture me
like a snare.

Her memories,
neither alive nor buried,
question me.

Yet remain,
a haunting,
secret.

# The Riots (2011)

I am the looter,
masked in dark despair,
taking to the streets,
stealing my fair share.

I am the banker,
dressed in city gear,
rolling in the green,
calculating fear.

I am the copper,
draped in riot blue,
fighting bricks and stones,
keeping calm but true.

I am the shop girl,
garbed in gory dress,
sweeping the high street,
hiding my distress.

I am the member,
clothed in summer wear,
weighing every word.
shaming all who care.

I am the justice,
robed in courtly black,
waving all the rules,
bringing solace back.

I am the dead man,

shrouded in old lies,
weeping in heaven,
whispering goodbyes.

I am the poet,
attired in cheap rhyme,
searching for answers,
serenading crime.

# Plea

Please come home,
April Jones.

Streets are safe,
free to roam.

Red tops chase
their new waif.

Killer's gone,
locked-in space.

Mum just waits,
watching phones.

Please come home,
April Jones.

# Dressed to Kill

Peacetime man, wartime plan,
you put me so at ease. I love
the style of what you wear,
you always dress to please.

Rip apart my insides
in sporty green fatigues.
Drop pink pills in my drink,
tie me up to please.

Chain me to your wall
of shame, mask your hate
with tease. Chase me down half-lit
streets, murder me in the trees.

Bring your gang to the feast,
copper-blue if you please.
Slay me in my marriage bed,
you put me so at ease.

Peacetime man, wartime plan
you give me such a thrill. I love
the guile of what you wear,
you always dress to kill.

# Seduction

Children echo in our hearts - name, age,
country - numbered for slaughter,
now mere candles in a hall of horrors.

Your Israeli tears for one such beloved
wet the Tikva streets we walk, pool in
Jerusalem's ancient alleyways of blood.

I am singing Leonard's raincoat song,
you wonder what he would think.
We wail at walls alongside bowing

holy men with their scribbled papers.
Yards away, Jesus' pilgrims kiss
his sacred stone, while teenage darlings,

their rucksacks sagging, keep their rifles
half-cocked. Flying out of Tel Aviv's
soulless airport, I plan to seduce you,

to rub precious Dead Sea ointment
into your weary feet. I hold you
through the Geneva night

but no tears, no songs, no wailing,
no amount of fucking
will bring the children back.

# Watching TV
*after Neil Postman*

We don't hear the rockets screaming
like dying men, smell the dark
clotted blood drenching desert sand.

And we don't see the rivers running red,
the skulls cracked open like eggs
littering village roads.

Instead, we carefully press the remote
when news interrupts our soaps.
Or mute *Two soldiers... killed today...*

*scores of civilians dead...*
change our synaptic channels
to keep amusing ourselves to death.

# Lee Rigby

Fresh blood
warms London's
trampled street.

Old hate
paints pavement
under feet.

New love
bursts with bouquets
in receipt.

Dry bones
run a rabid
fool's retreat.

# Go Now

Go now to peace.

The men have gone to war,
the children all are buried
beneath this bloody floor.

Go now to peace.

Mother's scarred and torn,
the rivers have run dry,
creation's time to mourn.

Go now to peace.

The women wait in vain.
The poppies have been planted,
we pray for acrid rain.

Go now to peace.

Wind grows silent as the night,
promises are fractured,
we must prepare for flight.

Go now to peace.

# Jigsaw Jesus

The church has gone pandemic,
they've closed her holy doors.

The saints are now just shut-ins,
so fewer ungodly wars.

They're Zooming into heaven,
as the online choir roars.

And I'm here self-isolating,
yes, bent down on all fours.

Worshipping jigsaw Jesus,
here on Broadstairs' divine shores.

# Sides of Heaven
*after Kris Kristofferson*

On the darker side of heaven
where they loot your very soul,
days without my inking body,
surely take a heavy toll.

On bended knee now for a poem,
trying to write away the wrong,
give me hell if I can't sing it,
take me back when it's a song.

If you want to get to earth now,
scatter letters one by one.
Put them back into your pocket,
or you'll never see the sun.

On the brighter side of heaven,
broken bodies become whole.
All those whispers in the morning,
wordless phrases that I stole.

# Grey Bishop
*for Rowan Williams*

at the gate, can't wait
to escape the long division,
forget holy states of schism.

It's time to search
bookish wisdom, to sing
equality's anthem –

Canterbury's behind him.
Good priest, goodbye,
sit this one out, though

wise with words he's lost
his clout. Grey bishop's
gate is left swinging.

# Death of a Theologian
*for James Reimer*

No time to pack those learned papers
proving You exist. A theologian's
heart stops short of truth.

Finding heaven is a galaxy
of big bangs. And You, a knot
of a god curled into a chair,

talking like Dell, telling me
there is no Maker. Only gases,
molecules, science guys.

Explaining my research
has black holes. That I had somehow
created the unfathomable.

# Good Friday

Dust clots and chokes
the unholy air, and the dry words
of white-haired men

in black cassocks whisper
through pious beards
within a shrouded monument

on God's sacred heath
commemorating, not the death
of Jesus, but his bloody church.

# Pressing Matters

Dylan's railin on the radio
bout all the rain that's gonna
fall on me.

I'm pressing on the steam button,
making rose-coloured pillow slips
into perfect squares.

The poet keeps groanin
bout kids with guns and swords,
folks laughin at the hunger around.

I'm ironing, lily-white bed sheets,
keeping all my lines
straight.

Bob's half-talkin, half-singin
bout highways of hate, rivers rife
with poison.

My new blue shirt
with bright white buttons
is now sleek as a politician's.

The prophet's doin an encore
bout forgotten souls,
more hard rain.

I turn off the radio, make my bed,
check the perfect image in the mirror,
don't care how hard it's raining.

# Orlando
*for William*

Good night, dear companion,
your morning struggle's done.
Oh, dear, but it's hard,
this sadness now begun.

Though good friends distract me –
they loved you without doubt –
after twenty years together,
God knows I want to shout.

Of warm and perfect evenings,
cuddled in your furry coat.
Still, I'd be forever grateful,
for music from your feline throat.

Good night, sweet Orlando,
no more games of hide and seek.
My days have lost their meaning,
at night my heart grows weak.

# I Want to Tell You

how scared I am
watching you daily strip away
like peels of onion skin,
baring your desperate soul.

Instead, I let myself
get distracted, with the hours
we spend over tortured
chicken breasts

in red wine sauce –
you spill on the white
tablecloth – exposing
the deep rupture in our politics.

I want to tell you how
I love you – platonic of course -
knowing even if we were lovers,
there's not an ounce of the carnal
left for craving.

Instead, I've let your looks
and your flirtations flow,
like the thin smoke
of your bones.

I want to tell you how
I pray, day and night,
for your emaciated emancipation.

Instead, I preach at your talk
of heaven, saying – this is
the only world that counts.

I want to tell you
how I admire the brutal beauty
of your haunted heart.

Instead, we salivate over
movie stars we'd most like to bed –
Julie Christie, and that un-pious priest in Fleabag.

I want to tell you how
I fear your relentless pursuit
of freedom, your slipping
away on silken wings.

Instead, I listen to you wax
your jokes about defying death,
all the while, all these years,
wanting to tell you – there will be
no exhortations, no goodbyes.

Instead, I am silent.

# Eve

Don't fret for me,
I'm grand, you see,
dancing now with angels.

Don't mourn for me,
I'm sipping tea,
in the company of angels.

Don't pray for me,
I'm lithe and free,
spinning round with angels.

Don't follow me,
keep your diary,
too soon to dance with angels.

# Waiting for Joe to Die

Morning light lifts a veil of grief
from Petit Sacconex Cemetery
where I've walked with you, my love,
whispering between tombstones and tulips,
wondering at the private mysteries
of these sleeping, grave-bound souls.

It would be the place to go now, but
you're high in a sleek Tokyo hotel tower,
without name or telephone number. So,
I welcome the early sun at my Geneva window,
wait for the crackly call from Ontario,
to tell me of my baby brother, Joe.

Then I'm back in the narrow alleyways
and patchy yards of our Toronto boyhood,
us being Jims again, sporting blue caps,
riding red tricycles, cops chasing robbers,
sailors following sudsy rivers
down the curb of our sometimes bloody street.

We build fortress sandcastles, cruise
the lakefront, catch sight of bare-skinned girls,
then build bonfires to light the dark and curl
our hungry bodies to their sweet warmth.
My brother Joe – beside me, part of me,
my constant ally, my gentle shadow.

We marry foolishly young, both of us,
and where Joe finds an understanding love,
a warm and sacred place, I look away,

run to exotic places, open spaces. Still,
long-distance calls and infrequent beers
bring us back to our boyhood bond.

Years later, while holidaying together
he pulls me from his treasured
Muskoka River, and my utter vanity.
We swim in cold lakes and deep pools,
yet somehow over time, we drift – I across
an ocean, he to a sodden sadness.

I wish you were back from Tokyo, my love,
so that I could hold you and tell you
about growing up with Joe, the brother
who helped make me, who floats now
above his gentle river, no longer chasing
but watching, wondering if it remembers him.

# Sweet Brother

*for Tommy*

Sweet brother Tommy,
slipping gently away
from love of the close ones,
and the light of the day.

Sweet brother Tommy,
slipping gently away
from the struggle of this harsh place,
the pain of the fray.

Sweet brother Tommy,
slipping gently away
to a place that is better,
where there is rest, we pray.

# Pity

I am too heavy for the sea,
too pale for you to spot me.

Thank God for the rocks
in my pockets. I sink

to this damp floor, but can't
die on this Kent shore.

Blue bobbies in hi-vis,
wake me to ask:

Were you dying?
I was trying.

Your name, sir?
Your city?

I don't know.
Such a pity.

# Longing

I don't need sunshine.
I don't need rain.
I don't need white wine.
I don't need pain.

I'm just longing for a longer night.

I don't need red meat.
I don't need French bread.
I don't need cakes sweet.
I don't need words said.

I'm just longing for a longer night.

I don't need bright lights.
I don't need gloom.
I don't need fist fights.
I don't need tomb.

I'm just longing for a longer night.

I don't need rhyming.
I don't need free.
I don't need climbing.
I don't need ski.

I'm just longing for a longer night.

I don't need church bells.
I don't need Book.
I don't need hard sells.

I don't need look.

I'm just longing for a longer night.

I don't need riches.
I don't need goods.
I don't need stitches.
I don't need shoulds.

I'm just longing for a longer night.

I don't need kisses.
I don't need hugs.
I don't need misses.
I don't need shrugs.

I'm just longing for a longer night.

I don't need lover.
I don't need crowd.
I don't need cover.
I don't need loud.

I'm just longing for a longer night.

# The Clinic

You brought me to the clinic, buried
in the bowels of gleaming King's Hospital,
told me there was no one else
you would rather have on this journey.

It has one of those crushing machines
that take snapshots of your breasts,
creating images a million miles from
those I've loved in our dim bedroom light.

Before nuking your flesh,
scorching and scarring
your perfect form beyond redemption.
White coats hush their gossip,

carrying on at work as if in
some airless office, not ground zero
for the chosen. Middle-aged women
fix worried eyes on weathered

magazines filled with dreams
of blissful country homes.
It's hospital-quiet, but the drop
of a shoulder, arch of an eyebrow,

a red mark on a sheet of paper,
punctuate the stillness. We navigate
bright corridors, finding the exit
out of this morbid edifice, saving

our whispers and embraces

for the street. I don't need to tell you,
you're the last person I want
to spend time with at such a clinic.

# Such a Night as This

Morning washes the night's brooding doubt.
What could the darkness have been all about?

Sun on my skin, on daylight's flowers,
casting out demons from the dangerous hours.

The moon brings my troubles, the stars despair,
the scent of your soul, the brush of your hair.

The morning is safe, no more reason to fret,
and remember the shadows – that's where we met.

# Blood

I cannot stomach the new tone
of my vintage blood, all rich in irony
after so many late-night draughts
and dramas, those sedentary Sundays,
and thick thatches of gateau galore.

Now my corpuscles are lab-bound,
where skinny kids in white coats
point their scopes at maps
of cancerous canals, and deep inside
their flow, I am drowning.

They log my stats then slip
outside to drag on sleek cigarettes,
to beam into the screens of their
young lives, to make weekend dates
on their stupid smart phones.

# Old Man Waiting

He sits quiet and alone,
trying to remember past mates.

Folks stroll by his sad wooden bench,
the wild sea beckons but he waits.

Some old friends went away to war,
others stayed close to garden gates.

He daydreams old loves and losses,
a life of regretting sad fates.

Sin offered him, accepted on whim,
blessings he mistook for weights.

He whispers prayers to God above,
washing his soul clean of bad states.

To everything new, he bids adieu,
forgetting life's poetic traits.

Old man sits quietly alone,
trying to remember past mates.

Folks stroll by his sad empty bench,
waving as he swims in dire straits.

# This Grey Age

What now,
at this grey age?

When still
chasing after wind.

While soul
springs with discontent.

Where heart's
more chuffed than chaste.

Who's left,
but this wizened one.

What now,
at his grey age?

But toil
of ancient rage.

Not just
for failing frame,

but soul's
fast fading dreams,

the corpse
that hides within.

# On the Wane

I read it in the flecks of fruit,
in my morning flakes of grain.

I didn't pass to altered states,
despite the grievous pain.

There's ringing in my ear drums,
it's driving me quite insane.

I fight for breath, sometimes it fails,
as the shock goes to my brain.

My gums are raw, my teeth they ache,
I spit blood into the drain.

I thought I had a heart attack,
but woke up where I'd lain.

They say it's all just in my head,
but for me it's very plain,

in just months I'll be sixty,
my temple is on the wane.

# On My Mrs No Longer Dyeing Her Hair

She issues her warning,
on a grey winter's morning,

this lady's for turning,
her brown locks she's spurning.

Take heed and take cover,
you must if you love her,

her white hair is growing,
revolution is blowing.

# Poem for Joyce Boyd

Wisdom and laughter
became lovers, birthing you.

You clothed yourself
in their vestments,
giving God an earthly face.

Your counsel burst,
like fountains of heavenly frolic.

Your joyful ripples echoed
like Sophia's words.
In your wisdom and laughter

we found God.
And we thank this God
for you.

# Babysitting

Waltzing with Jo-Eva on a Saturday night.
Dancing with the baby in the pale Paquis light.

Talking with Jo-Eva, all pink and quite a sight.
Singing with the baby, it gave her quite a fright.

Playing with Jo-Eva, while nanna takes her flight.
Crawling with the baby, we're trying not to fight.

Crying with Jo-Eva, she holds you oh so tight.
Sobbing with the baby, she wails with all her might.

Quieting down Jo-Eva, her eyes close just right.
Snoozing next to the baby, praying she'll be alright.

# Nothing

There's nothing between us,
save the spectacles hanging from your neck.

They keep us apart,
or tied up in knots.

And you can't see,
can barely see –

where my lips are.

There's nothing between us,
save the crucifix hanging from my neck.

It keeps us apart,
or tied up in plots.

And I can't feel,
can barely feel –

where your lips are.

There is nothing between us,
save these wretched rags.

They keep us apart,
or tied up in thoughts.

And we can't imagine,
can barely imagine –

where our lips are.

# Tenderly

Tenderly, tenderly,
all through the night.

Tenderly, tenderly,
take not your flight.

Tenderly, tenderly,
the morning is bright.

Tenderly, tenderly,
oh, what a sight.

Tenderly, tenderly,
take away the fright.

Tenderly, tenderly,
with all of your might.

Tenderly, tenderly,
making it right.

# Eighteen Short Poems of Absence

One
    It is your lips
    that waken me,
    electric
    on my skin,
    pulling me inside you,
    whispering love
    in your blue bed the morning you leave me,
    then on your mobile from the Geneva airport,
    and again from Amsterdam,
    and, I imagine, on the long, dark flight to Taipei.

Two
    I have discovered
    there are two kinds of time -
    the time that races,
    stealing the days and nights of you,
    and the time
    that grinds slowly,
    without you.

Three
    I know what time it is
    in Taipei
    every moment of the day.
    I count each minute
    until your return.

Four
    Create a sentence using the words poet and healthy.
    The healthy poet wrote nothing.

Five
    Do you hear it,
    in the crackling phone line
    from Taipei?
    Can you read it, between the lines,
    of the message I sent you –
    the irony of love,
    Leonard's disease,
    that makes me want to weep
    for the absence of you?

Six
    Emotional Intelligence is an oxymoron.

Seven
    Your voice is zen
    on the telephone.
    I hear your love.
    I sleep.

Eight
    Why don't you call me?
    Why don't you answer my calls?
    I curse the technology
    that robs me of your confidence.

Nine
    Ask me again
    if I ever cry…

Ten
    I shake
    all day
    from not sleeping at night.

Eleven
I feel you,
in our bed,
taste you on the pillow,
pour your oil on my body.
And rest,
assured by
your touch.

Twelve
I clean the footprints
from your bathtub,
the tea stains
from your kitchen,
try to detach from this need (is it such a bad thing,
I believe in the inter-dependence of people and nations, don't
I?),
this fear (one would be crazy not to fear the world, wouldn't
one?),
of the unknown.
I curse your strength,
and the certainty
of your soul
that I imagine sends you head-first down water wells,
seeking I know not what,
or dancing
with a sleek Hong Kong businessman
in the dark corner
of a Taipei karaoke bar,
while I weep
in the dark night
of my soullessness.

Thirteen
 I build an altar,
 with your red roses,
 and candles,
 your photograph,
 the one we all love.
 You are so thoughtful,
 beautiful,
 confident.
 You would be mortified by my worship.

Fourteen
 I kiss your photograph
 goodnight.

Fifteen
 Is it weak to call,
 weak to wait?
 Strong to call,
 strong to wait?
 I do not know.

Sixteen
 I eat alone.
 at a favourite restaurant,
 and the food
 is a cancer
 in my stomach.
 The Irish pub
 has lost its charm.
 Your Paquis streets are dirty.
 Your flat is stuffy.

Seventeen
I wish
I had used this time
to prepare
for the disappointment.
Remember
that night in the glow of candles and wine,
how I waxed on about my love
for you?
Remember?
You said,
I hope
I don't
disappoint
you.
I wish I had used this time to prepare.
It is something
your friends seem to be telling me
by their gentle looks.
Do they know
it is only a matter of time?
I wish I had used this time to prepare.

Eighteen
I am holding you,
your luggage at our feet,
our eyes fixed,
until our lips marry.
Don't let go…Don't let go…Don't let go…Don't let go…
Don't let go…Don't let go…Don't.

# Whispers
*for Michael and Claire*

Listen!

Can you hear it?

What is it?

Whispers.

From the back row?

No, ancient echoes off these holy walls.

What are they saying?

'I do, I do.'

'I can, I will.'

'I want to.'

'Love. You.'

\*\*\*

Listen!

Can you hear them?

Whispers again?

Yes.

'Ah, the bride, she's so beautiful.'

'A good woman.'

'Yes, a strong family too.'

'And the groom, he's so tall, and handsome.'

'A fine man.'

'And we know his family too, pillars of the community.'

\*\*\*

Listen!

Whispers again?

Yes, can you hear them?

From the back row?

No.

From the ancient whiskers and stiff collar in the pulpit.

What's he saying?

'There is a season … a time to embrace.'

Is that all?

No.

He's chanting.

'Love is patient, love is kind
rejoices in truth
bears all
believes all
hopes all
endures all things.'

\*\*\*

Listen!

Can you hear it?

What is it?

Mumbling.

From the back row?

No.

From the back centuries?

Not necessarily.

What are they saying?

'That's just Bible - stories.'

'No one believes it.'

'It's impossible.'

\*\*\*

Listen!

Can you hear it?

What is it now?

It's louder.

Who is it now?

Ancestors.

From the back row?

No.

From all round us, in the stone walls, in the stained glass.

Women and men who have knelt in this place and whispered.

What are they saying?

'You are not alone.'

Is that all?

And.

'God is with you.'

***

Listen.

Can you hear it?

Whispers.

From back the centuries?

No.

Today.

From the back row?

No.

From the front of the church. The couple.

What are they saying?

'I do, I do.'

'I can.'

'I will.'

'I want to.'

'Love. You.'

\*\*\*

Listen.

Can you hear it?

What is it, for God's sake?

Roaring.

From the back row?

No.

From every corner of the church!

What are they saying?

They are shouting.

What?

'Amen.'

# Crushed

That crimson blush,
that bloody rush
that fateful crush.

You're just in time,
you're looking fine,
your poems rhyme.

That scribbled word,
that love unheard,
that hope absurd.

# Appetite for Love

Sometimes I eat lunch – chicken, tomato,
brown bread – then alternate between
me and you, by sitting at both sides
of our makeshift kitchen table,
the white cloth marked by petals, tortoises,
and a tea stain (I'll have to explain).

I devour the meaty sandwich
(as you would) from your seat, looking
north towards white cliffs, shrouded
in mist and mystery. Then shift
to my place, dawdling over the remains
of my meal, banana and orange juice.

It's because you're travelling again,
so, I must nourish this ongoing dialogue.
I get the words right – *How are you, love?*
*I'm fine, tell me about the morning* –
but somehow, without you, I mess the tone,
the taste of love's delicious discourse.

# Acknowledgements

I am deeply grateful for the poetic wisdom of my editor, Vicky Morris, who remained supportive throughout the writing, re-writing, editing and publication process.

Thank you also to my first readers: Michael Sargent, Jeff Warren, Brian Clover, Ann Gallagher and Pat Hughes.

*Venice*, *Blood* and *Good Friday* first appeared in Current Accounts, published by The Bank Street Writers, Bolton.

*Bishop's Gate, Death of a Theologian, Body and Soul* and *On the Wane* first appeared in Inclement: Poetry for the Modern Soul.

As ever, I am blessed with the love and companionship of Pat Hughes, who loves poetry, and a poet.

www.ingramcontent.com/pod-product-compliance
Lightning Source LLC
La Vergne TN
LVHW041233080426
835508LV00011B/1185